I'm A Teacher

What's Your Super Power?

Over 100 lightly ruled pages for lesson plans,
reminders, journaling, and note taking.

A Notebook/Journal for
Inspirational Thoughts

ISBN-13: 978-1541274259

ISBN-10: 1541274253

RWSquaredMedia.Wordpress.com

A teacher takes a hand, opens a mind, and touches a heart.

A good education can change anyone. A good
teacher can change everything.

Teaching is the profession that teaches all of the other professions.

A teacher effects eternity. He can never tell where his influences stops.

A teacher takes a hand, opens a mind, and touches a heart.

A good education can change anyone. A good
teacher can change everything.

Teaching is the profession that teaches all of the other professions.

A teacher effects eternity. He can never tell where his influences stops.

A teacher takes a hand, opens a mind, and touches a heart.

A good education can change anyone. A good
teacher can change everything.

Teaching is the profession that teaches all of the other professions.

A teacher effects eternity. He can never tell where
his influences stops.

A teacher takes a hand, opens a mind, and touches a heart.

A good education can change anyone. A good teacher can change everything.

Teaching is the profession that teaches all of the other professions.

A teacher effects eternity. He can never tell where his influences stops.

A teacher takes a hand, opens a mind, and touches a heart.

A good education can change anyone. A good
teacher can change everything.

Teaching is the profession that teaches all of the other professions.

A teacher effects eternity. He can never tell where his influences stops.

A teacher takes a hand, opens a mind, and touches a heart.

A good education can change anyone. A good
teacher can change everything.

Teaching is the profession that teaches all of the other professions.

A teacher effects eternity. He can never tell where his influences stops.

A teacher takes a hand, opens a mind, and touches a heart.

A good education can change anyone. A good teacher can change everything.

Teaching is the profession that teaches all of the other professions.

A teacher effects eternity. He can never tell where his influences stops.

A teacher takes a hand, opens a mind, and touches a heart.

A good education can change anyone. A good
teacher can change everything.

Teaching is the profession that teaches all of the other professions.

A teacher effects eternity. He can never tell where his influences stops.

A teacher takes a hand, opens a mind, and touches a heart.

A good education can change anyone. A good
teacher can change everything.

Teaching is the profession that teaches all of the other professions.

A teacher effects eternity. He can never tell where his influences stops.

A teacher takes a hand, opens a mind, and touches a heart.

A good education can change anyone. A good
teacher can change everything.

Teaching is the profession that teaches all of the other professions.

A teacher effects eternity. He can never tell where his influences stops.

_____
_____
_____
_____
_____
_____
_____
_____
_____
_____
_____
_____
_____
_____
_____
_____
_____
_____
_____
_____
_____
_____
_____

A teacher takes a hand, opens a mind, and touches a heart.

A good education can change anyone. A good
teacher can change everything.

Teaching is the profession that teaches all of the other professions.

A teacher effects eternity. He can never tell where his influences stops.

A teacher takes a hand, opens a mind, and touches a heart.

A good education can change anyone. A good
teacher can change everything.

Teaching is the profession that teaches all of the other professions.

A teacher effects eternity. He can never tell where his influences stops.

A teacher takes a hand, opens a mind, and touches a heart.

A good education can change anyone. A good
teacher can change everything.

Teaching is the profession that teaches all of the other professions.

A teacher effects eternity. He can never tell where his influences stops.

A teacher takes a hand, opens a mind, and touches a heart.

A good education can change anyone. A good
teacher can change everything.

Teaching is the profession that teaches all of the other professions.

A teacher effects eternity. He can never tell where his influences stops.

A teacher takes a hand, opens a mind, and touches a heart.

A good education can change anyone. A good
teacher can change everything.

Teaching is the profession that teaches all of the other professions.

A teacher effects eternity. He can never tell where his influences stops.

A teacher takes a hand, opens a mind, and touches a heart.

A good education can change anyone. A good
teacher can change everything.

Teaching is the profession that teaches all of the other professions.

A teacher effects eternity. He can never tell where his influences stops.

A teacher takes a hand, opens a mind, and touches a heart.

A good education can change anyone. A good
teacher can change everything.

Teaching is the profession that teaches all of the other professions.

A teacher effects eternity. He can never tell where his influences stops.

A teacher takes a hand, opens a mind, and touches a heart.

A good education can change anyone. A good
teacher can change everything.

Teaching is the profession that teaches all of the other professions.

A teacher effects eternity. He can never tell where his influences stops.

A teacher takes a hand, opens a mind, and touches a heart.

A good education can change anyone. A good
teacher can change everything.

Teaching is the profession that teaches all of the other professions.

A teacher effects eternity. He can never tell where his influences stops.

A teacher takes a hand, opens a mind, and touches a heart.

A good education can change anyone. A good
teacher can change everything.

Teaching is the profession that teaches all of the other professions.

A teacher effects eternity. He can never tell where his influences stops.

A teacher takes a hand, opens a mind, and touches a heart.

A good education can change anyone. A good
teacher can change everything.

Teaching is the profession that teaches all of the other professions.

A teacher effects eternity. He can never tell where his influences stops.

A teacher takes a hand, opens a mind, and touches a heart.

A good education can change anyone. A good
teacher can change everything.

Teaching is the profession that teaches all of the other professions.

A teacher effects eternity. He can never tell where his influences stops.

A teacher takes a hand, opens a mind, and touches
a heart.

A good education can change anyone. A good
teacher can change everything.

Teaching is the profession that teaches all of the other professions.

A teacher effects eternity. He can never tell where his influences stops.

A teacher takes a hand, opens a mind, and touches a heart.

A good education can change anyone. A good
teacher can change everything.

Teaching is the profession that teaches all of the other professions.

A teacher effects eternity. He can never tell where his influences stops.

A teacher takes a hand, opens a mind, and touches a heart.

A good education can change anyone. A good
teacher can change everything.

Teaching is the profession that teaches all of the other professions.

A teacher effects eternity. He can never tell where his influences stops.

A teacher takes a hand, opens a mind, and touches a heart.

A good education can change anyone. A good
teacher can change everything.

Teaching is the profession that teaches all of the other professions.

A teacher effects eternity. He can never tell where his influences stops.

For more amazing journals and adult coloring books from RW Squared Media, visit:

Amazon.com
CreateSpace.com
RWSquaredMedia.Wordpress.com

The Adult Coloring Book for
Coffee Lovers

The Ultimate Adult Coloring Book
for Men

Cities of the World Coloring Book
for Adults

Wine, Cheese, Crackers, and Coloring

Made in the USA
Lexington, KY
23 May 2017